Original title:
The Necklace in the Dark

Copyright © 2025 Creative Arts Management OÜ
All rights reserved.

Author: Thomas Sinclair
ISBN HARDBACK: 978-1-80586-140-9
ISBN PAPERBACK: 978-1-80586-612-1

Echoes of a Luminous Past

In shadows flicker memories bright,
Of sparkles lost in the moonlight.
A treasure once graced a neck so fair,
Now it's just tales, floating in air.

With laughter echoing off the walls,
As dreams of riches take their falls.
A heist of glamour, a slip in the night,
Oh, who knew brilliance could take flight?

In corners hide whispers of gleam,
While giggles dance, a curious theme.
Gemstones stolen, what a delight,
Who needs jewels when jesters ignite?

So raise a toast to what once shone,
To laughter shared, though riches are gone.
In a world where fun can blend and thrive,
Our memories sparkle, forever alive.

Unraveled Elegance

In a box, it lay, so grand,
A twist of fate in a nervous hand.
The dinner party came with a twist,
But where's the charm? Hold on, I insist!

She wore her flair like a bold disguise,
While laughter echoed, she faked surprise.
A twinkling bling that stole the show,
Yet it vanished fast—oh no, oh no!

The Allure of Concealed Brilliance

Behind the curtain, whispers spread,
That shining treasure, a stolen thread.
With clinking glasses, they danced all night,
While she had doubts, but felt so light.

A glittering secret, oh what a glow,
To dazzle friends, but did they know?
As shadows waltzed, a sly charade,
Her laughter masked a great charade.

Shadows That Sparkle

In the moonlight dim, it sparkled bright,
An evening mishap gave quite a fright.
With each step taken, she felt the thrill,
But fate, it seems, had other plans still.

As shadows danced with a cheeky flair,
The charming glow vanished in thin air.
Where did it go? Was it smoke, or mirth?
The audience laughed; she felt the dearth.

Secrets of Gilded Night

At midnight's hour, a raucous cheer,
Gilded secrets twinkled near.
In the dark, they played their game,
While she giggled, forgetting her name.

A slide and a stumble, a hilarious shun,
While jewels hide—oh, what fun!
Her charm unravels, yet spirits hold tight,
For every mishap, a legendary night!

Metaphors of Midnight's Grace

In shadows deep, I trip and fall,
A sparkle bright, I can't recall.
With laughter loud, I search around,
For gems that hide beneath the ground.

A rogue in night, I strut and sway,
Chasing glimmers that dance away.
My pockets light, but heart aglow,
For every laugh, I steal the show.

Darkness's Silent Brilliance

When night does cloak the bustling street,
I find my joy in stumbling feet.
A twinkle here, a chuckle there,
In the velvet void, I've none to spare.

Like moths to flame, we drift and dive,
In silken night, we feel alive.
With whispers shared and secrets spun,
Who knew that shadow could be such fun?

Lost in a Sea of Glint

Round every corner, a flash I seek,
A hidden treasure makes me weak.
With eager hands, I fumble through,
For sparkles tucked where none construe.

The midnight cheer, a silly game,
Each shiny thing just screams my name.
In laughter shared under moonlit shade,
Who knew this joy would never fade?

A Portrait of Dusk's Luster

As day dips low, and colors blend,
I paint with giggles, my newest trend.
With starlit dots and moonbeam streaks,
In twilight's glow, I'm bold, I peak.

Amidst the fun, I weave a tale,
Of shining mischief and a clumsy quail.
In dusk's embrace, I laugh so hard,
For life's bright jewels are this night's card.

Treasures Hidden from the Light

In a drawer, secrets wait,
Hiding from the light of fate.
Sparkles dusted with a sigh,
Whispers laugh as shadows fly.

Found a brooch, all crooked charms,
Jewels stolen from life's arms.
Worn on days that feel so drab,
Like a joke without a gab.

Laughter echoes in the gloom,
As a shirt button becomes the bloom.
Fashion faux pas gone astray,
Just a shimmer that dances away.

Glittering treasures, one or two,
Actually bits of toast and glue.
In the dark, they tickle one's heart,
Who knew that style was such an art?

Radiance Beneath the Veil

Underneath a slight disguise,
Lies a plethora of surprise.
A tiara made of fuzzy socks,
Shimmering bright like silly clocks.

Rummaging through things unkempt,
Jewel-toned spaghetti – heaven's spent!
Wrapped in laughter, a cheerful play,
In shadows where the jokesters stay.

A mirror shines with honeyed grace,
Reflecting a truly goofy face.
Gems and beads from last year's craft,
Make even boredom take a laugh.

Twinkling under every fold,
Are memories worth more than gold.
A dance ensues, the night grows wild,
In the dark, remain forever child.

Chasing Glimmers of Midnight

In the night, a glint appears,
Chasing shadows without fears.
An old shoe gleams, a silver star,
Tipped by laughter, near and far.

With a leaf stuck to a crown,
Wearing it like a jester's gown.
Twirling thoughts of what might be,
In the dark, hilarious glee.

Banana peels and diamonds fake,
Are the treasures that we take.
Each step echoes with a jest,
Joyful glimmers overspread the rest.

Underneath the crazy moon,
Dancing to a silly tune.
Laughter spills, the night delight,
Chasing glimmers till first light.

Echoes of Silent Elegance

In the quiet, elegance sneaks,
While sensible, the silly speaks.
A fancy hat with feathers bright,
Makes the mundane take flight.

Woven tales of socks and shoes,
Are the hidden, fun-filled clues.
On grand stages, antics be,
Where silence laughs hysterically.

Charming china, chipped with pride,
Plays the role of shining guide.
Glistening laughter, echoes loud,
As nonsense dances through the crowd.

Whispers of grace in goofy ways,
Mark the night with humorous plays.
In the silence, sparkle gleams,
Woven through our wildest dreams.

Glisten of the Unknown

In shadows deep, a sparkle shines,
A treasure tucked 'neath tangled vines.
Who knew while laughing, it would be found,
A jewel that danced on the ground?

With every wink, it giggled bright,
Fooling those who trod at night.
A glow that flickers, hides, and seeks,
Like cats that chat in whispered speaks.

Radiant Whispers of the Night

What twirls in dark? A shimm'ring jest,
A playful glow that leaves you blessed.
Beneath the moon, it casts a bet,
On who will laugh, and who will fret.

Gems of giggles float like air,
Chasing shadows without a care.
With each gleam, a chuckle grows,
In the night, amidst the doze.

Eclipsed Beauty

A clever trickster in the gloom,
Winks at the world with leafy bloom.
It hides and seeks, a game of light,
Where laughter gleams, and moods feel bright.

In alleys dark, it glows and beams,
Whispering secrets, sharing dreams.
No one suspects the fun within,
A chuckle wrapped in a twinkling spin.

The Charm Within Darkness

What shines amidst the cloak of night?
A jester's grin, a silly sight.
It plays peek-a-boo with shadows tall,
Spreading joy, enticing all.

Each twinkle tells a funny tale,
Of mishaps caught in moonlight pale.
A charm that prances, leaps about,
In darkness, finds a joyful rout.

Dusk's Delicate Touch

As twilight falls, a shadow creeps,
A clumsy cat honks, and the laughter leaps.
The moon's a jester, winking with glee,
While stars spin tales, oh what a spree!

A glint from a box, or so we assume,
Turns out it's just a glow from the broom.
Gems shimmer in dreams, or so they say,
But all I found was my cat on display!

Opulence in Silence

In a room full of glitter, a party unfolds,
With whispers of riches, and secrets untold.
But as I glide in my rags with a grin,
I trip over shoes, let the awkward begin!

With chandeliers swinging, I wobble with charm,
Trying to dazzle, yet causing alarm.
The jokes on the jewels, for I'm quite a catch,
In a world full of class, I'm the not-so-smooth match!

Silent Sparkle

In the dead of night, a jewel might flicker,
Or was it just my flashlight? Oh, this gets trickier!
With each tiny glimmer, my heart starts to race,
But then it's just a chipmunk, with a mischievous face.

Caught in the sparkle, I dance all around,
Until I bump into a very soft mound.
I laugh at myself, in this playful charade,
It's a party for one, and I'm not getting paid!

Ethereal Adornment

Under the soft glow, I strut with glee,
Wearing my pearls, which are just baked peas.
Folks might not notice, but I'm feeling fine,
The humor lies there, in my veggie design!

I twirl and I promise I'm glittering bright,
But really, it's just my glow-in-the-dark light.
The laughter erupts, as my peas take a fall,
Dressed as I am, I still stand tall!

Threads of Enigma and Light

In shadows cast by brilliant spark,
A lost treasure waits to embark.
It twirls and glimmers, takes a flight,
Dancing whims in the soft twilight.

The cats conspire, oh what a sight,
Chasing gems with playful delight.
While I just sit, a bit bemused,
At all my trinkets, slightly confused.

Illusion sparkles, laughter's the key,
In the tangle of threads, fun is free.
A game of fate, a twist of chance,
Who needs riches when you have this dance?

A bangle here, a bracelet there,
Fashion disasters beyond compare.
Yet in the dark, the humor shines,
Even chaos can be so divine.

Dreams Shimmering in Obscurity.

In dreams we find lost glimmers bright,
As shadows play with sheer delight.
A whisper here, a giggle there,
In twilight's grip, we dance with flair.

My pocket's filled with shiny lies,
Oh, how they twinkle, what a surprise!
Like fireflies caught in tangled nets,
Each spark ignites, we're free from debts.

To chase a laugh in velvet dark,
A sparkle leads, igniting spark.
We wear our whims like hats of jest,
As absurdity puts fate to the test.

And in this haze, what do we find?
A treasure trove of the silly kind.
For echoes of joy, let laughter flow,
In dreams of dusk, we steal the show.

Glint of Midnight Gem

A glint of hope, a midnight gem,
Sits gleaming on a phantom stem.
Like socks that vanish without a trace,
This gem's allure is sheer embrace.

At every turn, the jesters call,
"Look at that shine! It's best of all!"
But laughter hides where secrets play,
In midnight's veil, they slip away.

One moment grand, the next a flop,
As humor reigns, we'll never stop.
To chase the luster, misunderstand,
In the dark, we'll make our stand.

So clutch those gems of silly dreams,
For in their light, nothing's as it seems.
And when the dawn breaks, we still will jest,
In playful whispers, we'll be blessed.

Whispered Elegance

With whispered tales of elegance,
A subtle charm, an odd romance.
In velvet night, the jesters glow,
Where all things fanciful freely flow.

A hat that's askew, a shoe that squeaks,
Our lives are woven with funny tweaks.
Each twist and turn, a tale unfurled,
In shadows bright, we spin our world.

So here's to gems that shine and fade,
To fashion blunders, unafraid!
In whispered elegance we shall sway,
Finding joy in the silliest way.

For in the dark, our laughter reigns,
A comedy wrapped in lovely chains.
So come join in this timeless spree,
Where elegance meets a clownish glee.

Echoes of Opulent Dark

In a shadowed room, laughter flies,
Where sparkles dance in sneaky lies.
A lady spins with flair so bright,
To flaunt her jewels, oh what a sight!

But under the weight of her grand tale,
Her purse grows light, it starts to pale.
With every swish, a fell gust blows,
Leaving her searching for shiny woes!

With a wink, her friends gather near,
To joke about gems, and sip some beer.
"Is it a diamond? Or just a stone?"
They giggle and chuckle in their tone.

At midnight's strike, the truth would crack,
That splendor isn't found, but comes from the lack.

Glistening Under Starlight

In the corner of a bustling bar,
A lady shines bright, like a shooting star.
With laughter bubbling and cheeks aglow,
She talks of riches, putting on a show.

But as she twirls and spins around,
She trips on her tales, and tumbles down.
Her friends all gasp but then they giggle,
As jewels roll about, oh what a wiggle!

"Do you see this pearl?" she grandly claims,
Only to find it's really a game.
A little marble from her son's play,
"Oh dear, it's still lovely, hip-hip-hooray!"

Yet in the sparkles of laughter shared,
The ladies now know they need not be scared.

The Weight of Radiance

A crown of sparkle sits high on a head,
But who knew it was all just thoughts instead?
Each flicker and glow, a story they'd weave,
Of treasures and riches in which they believe.

"Look at my baubles!" she proudly exclaims,
While friend whispers softly, "Those aren't real claims!"
A flick of the wrist and jewels go flying,
Down the street they roll; there's no denying!

With a scuffle, a laugh, the chase is on,
As friends claim the light in the softening dawn.
"Let's gather 'round, let's laugh and recount,
Our weight in gold is just in our flount!

A Gift Wrapped in Mystery

A present so grand, wrapped with flair,
Inside might be treasures, with luck to spare.
Unravel the layers, oh what will it be?
A gag or a gem, wait and see!

She gasps and she laughs, but what's in the box?
A rubber chicken or some shiny rocks?
With friends all around, they burst into cheers,
For all that they've opened are chuckles, not tears!

"So much fun!" she says with glee,
"It's more than a necklace, it's mystery!"
Together they tread through the night so stark,
Laughter as jewels in the chilly park.

Shadows of Adorned Secrets

In the closet, treasures sit,
Sparkling brightly, every bit.
Spy a trinket, it looks divine,
But oh, the tale—it's not just mine.

A hidden gem, in darkness slipped,
Life of glitz that I have gripped.
With a giggle, I tiptoe tight,
Nightly mischief under the light.

Whispers of bling, all giggles sway,
In my hands, they long to play.
Shadows dance, with humor bright,
Secrets shimmer in the night.

When morning comes, it's all a joke,
A laugh, a wink, my heart awoke.
For what's a jewel if not for fun?
In playful dreams, my wealth is spun.

Luminous Chains of Silence

Clinking jewels in moonlit gleam,
They twinkle, dance, and softly beam.
Whispers travel through the air,
Hiding secrets, unaware.

A charm is lost—where did it go?
On this quest, we search below.
Under starlight, giggles blend,
A spree of laughter, let's pretend.

The chains may shine, but oh, be wary,
For mischief waits, quite legendary.
With every laugh, another twist,
In this game, who could resist?

What's elegance without a jest?
In midnight glee, we find our rest.
With beads of humor, we delight,
Crafting stories in the night.

Hidden Glimmers

Beneath the bed, a secret spark,
A twinkle hides within the dark.
Curiosity pokes and prods,
As laughter escapes, from timid nods.

In toy boxes, jewels collide,
Whimsical tales refuse to hide.
With every glimmer, there's a jest,
In shadows soft, we're truly blessed.

Flashy dreams in cozy gloom,
Let's light the night with misfit bloom.
For who needs glam when fun ignites?
With sparkling whims, we claim our rights.

The hidden glimmers—sparkly fools,
In silly games, we make our rules.
Together lost, with no alarm,
Adventures whispers, full of charm.

Night's Veil of Beauty

Night falls softly, beauty's hue,
With laughter wrapped in each debut.
A silky veil, shadows dance,
Trinkets sparkle in chance romance.

What's that glimmer? A nod to fate,
In playful jest, we dare relate.
A game of hide and wink and run,
In the dark, we've only just begun.

Where moonlight falls, the laughs unfold,
A story crafted, gleefully bold.
Each jewel's laughter, each flicker grants,
In the silence, a jolly dance.

The beauty's there, though mischief stirs,
With each gleam, we make our blurs.
For in the dark, our spirits soar,
With every giggle, we'll ask for more.

Veins of Light Beneath Darkness

In a corner, lost with grace,
A trinket found, bright as a face.
It sparkles more than a cow's surprise,
A rubber chicken floors the wise.

Who needs gold when you have fun?
Wrapped in shadows, not to shun.
A puzzling charm, not quite so clear,
It tickles nerves and brings a cheer.

With humor stitched in threads so tight,
This bit of whimsy shines at night.
A treasure map, but what a blunder,
To chase a smile instead of thunder.

So wander on, through shades of mirth,
Where laughter dances, death finds birth.
In every glimmer, a secret hark,
Veins of light that fill the dark.

Beauty Cloaked in Night

A veil of shadows drapes the scene,
With giggles caught where none have been.
In midnight's hush, the echoes play,
Beauty lurks in a silly way.

A lopsided grin, a clownish glee,
A flurry of sparkles, wild and free.
A hodgepodge of wonders wrapped up tight,
Unruly jewels in the cloak of night.

Whispers of laughter brush the dark,
Like fireflies trapping a tiny spark.
With every twist and turn of fate,
A jest emerges, oh, how great!

In the dimness, comical sheen,
Where even the shadows dance and preen.
With beauty cloaked that won't be tamed,
The night chuckles, and life is flamed.

Jewels of the Shadowed Heart

Underneath the moon's own crown,
Lies a treasure, upside-down.
Glimmers of joy, satiric grace,
Funny moments claim the space.

A heart adorned with prankish flair,
Each shiny bead simply laid bare.
Nonsense prances with every beat,
A riddle dressed so very neat.

In pockets deep where giggles dwell,
A trove of quirks, like tales to tell.
Hearts can glimmer in the kooky dark,
Where laughter blooms and leaves its mark.

So delve into this playful night,
Jewels of folly bring delight.
In shadows deep, the heart reveals,
A world of humor, love, and squeals.

Velvet Riches

In velvet robes where laughter hides,
Riches flourish, enthusiasm rides.
An oddball charm, a playful tease,
Gems of joy float by with ease.

Fluttering around with snickers loud,
An odd arrangement, a quirk embraced.
What's wealth without a smirk to share,
With treasures made from silly flair?

Among the trinkets, giggles dance,
The joyful heart takes its stance.
Bright against all the mundane fuss,
Velvet riches laugh with us.

So gather close, and heed the call,
In the richness of laughter, we stand tall.
For what's more grand than fun as gold,
In a world of velvet, let joy unfold.

Midnight's Timeless Gems

In shadows, they play, oh what a sight,
Dancing on tables, till the morning light.
Stolen from dreams, they twinkle and tease,
Whispers of laughter drift through the breeze.

A pair of lost earrings, on a cat's tail,
Twirling in circles, a humorous trail.
They jingle and jive, a curious pair,
Gems of the night, without a care!

In the moon's gentle glow, they sparkle and leap,
While mortals below are slumbering deep.
They shine in such chaos, a comedy sparked,
These midnight treasures, so silly and marked.

With giggles they scatter, those trinkets so bright,
Causing mischief till the dawn's early light.
Sparkling with laughter, a whimsical tune,
Midnight's fair gems, they'll see you soon!

Reflections in the Abyss

In the depths of the night, they swim and wade,
Glimmers of jest in a watery parade.
Bubbles of laughter, they rise to the top,
Jokes of the sea that just never stop.

A mirror of splendor, a fish takes a dive,
Thinking it's handsome, it's quite the alive!
But lo! A seahorse with style so grand,
Dances by with a smirk, just as he planned.

Reflections of silly, so bright in the tide,
Who needs a crown when you can just glide?
Around and around, they swirl with delight,
The laughter echoes, echoing the night.

So gather ye treasures and dive into fun,
With giggles and gems, the night's just begun!
In the depths of the darkness, the splendor appears,
Reflections of joy that outshine your fears.

A Symphony of Starlit Jewels

Under a canopy of twinkling frames,
The stars join in on this laughter game.
A symphony plays with each glimmering wink,
Notes dancing softly, in sync they link.

A diamond slipped away to join in the fun,
Bouncing through shadows, oh what a run!
While pearls giggle quietly, rolling around,
Creating soft music, a magical sound.

With ruffles and shines, they move to and fro,
Whirling and twirling, stealing the show.
They spin the old tales of frolic and glee,
A delightful performance, oh can't you see?

Each jewel takes a turn, adding to the flair,
Creating a raucous and colorful air.
Under the night sky, with each laugh and jest,
A symphony of gems, truly the best!

Glimmers that Dance in Darkness

In the heart of the night, where the shadows reside,
Glimmers come forth, with nothing to hide.
Flickering lights that giggle and sway,
They throw their own party, come join the fray!

A sprinkle of humor, a dash of delight,
Each shiny bauble takes flight in the night.
With jests exchanged, they leap and they spin,
Proving the fun that lies deep within.

Bouncing on beams of enchanted moonlight,
These mischievous gems create splendid sights.
Joking with clouds as they drift overhead,
Each glimmery wink is like laughter well-spread.

So gather your joy, let the dark be your stage,
With glimmers so bright, you'll forget the age.
For life's little pleasures come wrapped in delight,
And dance through the darkness with all of your might!

Adornment of Anonymity

In shadows where secrets dwell,
A gem so bright, could cast a spell.
With laughter hiding behind the gleam,
A priceless laugh slips through the seam.

A splendid glow serves a wily tease,
Worn by those who float with ease.
A dazzling charm, a comical plight,
Hiding giggles in the moonlit night.

Secrets Coveted in Twilight

In the fall of dusk, whispers fly,
A shiny trinket, oh so sly!
Glimmers in corners, acting coy,
Teasing the heart, a mischievous joy.

As shadows dance and play their game,
The secret smiles hide their name.
With every sparkle, laughter swells,
Wrapped in a tale that no one tells.

The Riddle of Radiance

A riddle wrapped in gleaming charm,
With every glint, it spins its arm.
Who owns the shine beneath the veil?
In chuckles, we find the hidden trail.

The mystery tickles as it glows,
Where humor dwells, the intrigue grows.
A twinkle here, a jesting wink,
With every shine, our thoughts all link.

Stolen Dreams Reflecting Light

A dream once caught in sparkly threads,
Twirled and whirled in playful spreads.
The glow invites a silly chase,
As laughter flows and takes its place.

Forgotten wishes whirl about,
Glistening tales that make us shout.
In stolen moments, joy ignites,
Reflecting dreams in brilliant nights.

A Tale of Lost Brilliance

Once I had a gem, so bright,
Wore it out one fateful night.
But my dance was quite the scene,
Off it flew, oh how obscene!

Checked the floor and checked my bag,
All I found was an old rag.
Is it under the cat's tail?
Or lost in the ale-filled pail?

Thought I'd find it in the park,
But I tripped and hit the bark.
Now it's gone, oh what a shame,
Next time I'll just blame the fame!

Laughter echoes in my heart,
For the jewel, I'll never part.
But who could need a sparkly thing,
When mischief's what this night will bring?

Veiled Radiance at Dusk

Blinded by the glow so fine,
I wore my treasure, felt divine.
But during dinner, oh what fun,
Spilled my drink, and now it's done!

Each bite was full of such delight,
Until it vanished from my sight.
Was it fish, or between the bread?
Guess I'll wear my shame instead!

With the moon's light, I had a quest,
Searching hard, I must confess.
Looked beneath the dining chair,
But found old socks, not jewels rare!

Now I wear this empty bling,
And laugh at what the night could bring.
For in the laughs I find my grace,
Who needs gems when I've got this face?

Subtle Glows in the Gloaming

Out in the garden, gleaming bright,
Something sparkled in the night.
Thought I saw a glowing prize,
But it turned out to be flies!

Chasing glimmers, oh what fun,
Stumbling 'round, I lost my run.
Caught the dog with all my flair,
Now he thinks he's a millionaire!

The stars above laugh out loud,
As I bumble, chasing my crowd.
"Look, a fortune!" I would boast,
Oh, how I'm the laughing host!

Finally dropped on grass so soft,
And declared my treasure lost.
But in its place, I found a laugh,
That's worth more than a diamond's half!

Through the Cloak of Night

Sneaked out in the dead of night,
Hoping for a wondrous sight.
But tripped over my own two feet,
And landed flat—what a defeat!

Looked around for something grand,
Only found the moonlit sand.
Grabbed a sparkly pebble there,
Thought perhaps it was too rare!

Wore it proudly on my shirt,
But it turned out to be dirt!
Still, I strutted, feeling bold,
Claiming glories never told.

Friends now laugh over my plight,
Calling me the "Dirt-Rock Knight."
But deep inside, I still embrace,
Funny treasures make the grace!

Charmed Whispers

In shadows deep, a treasure gleams,
A fumble here, or so it seems.
With laughter echoes, secrets shared,
A clumsy dance, yet none are scared.

A sparkly fling, a silly prank,
It vanishes, oh, what a prank!
With giggles loud, they start the chase,
Who knew that jewels could leave a trace?

Behind the curtain, wit takes flight,
A shimmering twist in the moonlight.
In cozy nooks, they trade a grin,
For finding gems is where laughter begins.

So join the fun, let worries part,
With twinkling charms and a foolish heart.
Together we'll share this joyous spree,
As sparkling whispers set us free.

Enchantment Within Shadows

Once in a haze, the moonlight chuckled,
As silly souls around it snuggled.
With whispers held and laughter loud,
They pranced about, a jeweled crowd.

A twinkling charm, oh what a sight,
But oops! It slipped out into the night.
With shouts of glee, they scurry near,
For every glimmer holds a cheer!

As shadows dance, their secrets fly,
In splendid chaos beneath the sky.
With mischief wrapped in splendor's guise,
A wondrous tale, a pure surprise.

With every step, more giggles spill,
As whimsy gathers, it's such a thrill.
In shimmering darkness, hearts will sway,
For laughter brightens the wildest play.

A Dance of Hidden Jewels

Step to the side, a gleam appears,
With joyful smiles and twinkling cheers.
The socks mismatched, the shoes askew,
Yet where they're going, none has a clue.

They trip and stumble, a merry crew,
As laughter echoes, chase ensues.
A sparkly flash, oh, where'd it go?
Lost in the charm of a bright glow.

The moon's a witness to all the fun,
In this silly game, they're never done.
With hidden gems and witty lines,
They dance through stories, like aged vines.

In muddled paths where giggles bloom,
They'll whirl about, dispelling gloom.
A silly waltz in the starry night,
For in this joy, the heart takes flight.

Cloaked in Glamour

In glitzy folds and twinkling laughs,
The charm unfolds in twists and crafts.
A secret stash, or so it seems,
In pockets deep, where giggle beams.

A wobbly step, a sparkling face,
In every twirl, they find their place.
Through clumsy moves, the jokes abound,
As whispers play all around.

With glamour wrapped in joyous pranks,
Our heroes dance with silly flanks.
Hiding treasures in plain sight,
In grinning games that spark delight.

In this mischief, let's raise a cheer,
For laughter shines, it's crystal clear.
With every tangle, joy's true charm,
In comical tales, there's endless balm.

Whispers of Gemstone Shadows

In the attic's nook, a shiny bead,
Gathering dust, it begins to plead.
"I once sparkled bright, oh what a show,"
Now I hide here, where no one will go.

A squirrel stops by, wears it like a crown,
Pretending to rule the old, creaky town.
"Look at me now!" it chirps with delight,
As I chuckle and watch from my shadowy height.

Mice join in, clinking, a tiny parade,
Their disco ball dreams in the gloom displayed.
With fuzzy little feet, they dance on the floor,
In this gem-filled whispers, who could ask for more?

But as morning breaks, the party must wane,
Squirrels and mice now all sleepy and plain.
Back to my corner, I'll just rest for now,
Until night calls again, with its whimsical vow.

Luster Shrouded in Twilight

In darkened rooms where shadows play,
A flamboyant ring tucked far away.
"Oh, where's my sparkle?" it starts to cry,
As the cat walks by, with a wary eye.

The clock strikes twelve, and the laughter roars,
Who needs a gala with such fine decor?
While slippers squeak, and the floorboards groan,
This hidden treasure's preparing to moan.

A pair of socks, mismatched and bold,
Join the affair, both worn and cold.
They twirl and prance with gleeful grace,
Chasing gleams in this odd little space.

But alas! The sun peeks in with a grin,
And the home seems quiet where the fun has been.
Time slips away, but I'll keep my quirk,
In shadows of twilight, where secrets still lurk.

Adornments of the Unseen

A golden chain, tangled in fluff,
Sighs for the days when it was enough.
"I'm still fabulous!" it curls with pride,
But the mirror reflects a twisted ride.

The dog prances by, with a wink of fate,
Sporting a collar that's far from great.
But when it shakes, oh the noise and clink!
The house turns into a disco, I think!

Under the bed, a lost pendant lies,
With dust bunnies giving it shifty eyes.
"A party's a party," it starts to hum,
"Let's gather the lost, see what may come!"

Yet dawn approaches, and the sparkle must hide,
As the floors once again are swept aside.
Tomorrow, dear gems, we'll dance once more,
In antics of laughter, from ceiling to floor.

Secrets Worn Under Moonlight

Under the moon, a bracelet gleams,
Sharing wild tales, or so it seems.
"I once dazzled kings, now I'm under the bed,"
It laughs with the dust motes swirling ahead.

The broom comes swishing, a dancer in stride,
While the keys in the drawer passionately bide.
"Let's rattle and roll, make a spirited sound!"
In the whispering night, magic abounds.

A moth flutters close, adorned in delight,
Whispers of shimmer, lost in the night.
"Join us, dear friend!" the secrets all call,
As the laughter erupts in the dimmest of halls.

But the first rays of dawn send the shadows in flight,
The glamour retreats, receding from sight.
Yet under the surface, the whispers remain,
Waiting for evening to dance once again.

Hushed Beauty of the Nocturne

In shadows where the whispers play,
Gem glimmers with a cheeky sway.
Stars above roll their eyes, you see,
As moonlight giggles, wild and free.

A clumsy dance of sparkles bright,
Turns elegance to pure delight.
In velvet night, the mischief stirs,
With sneezes masked by flustered furs.

Laughter echoes in silent charms,
As heists unfold with playful arms.
What's lost can be a splendid jest,
The darkened beauty's hidden quest.

So here's to giggles underneath,
To treasures found in laughter's wreath.
For in this hush, a tale we weave,
Of sparkly dreams we all believe.

The Elegance of Obscurity

In shadows deep, a wink so sly,
A glinting charm beneath the sky.
With giggles shared in hushed delight,
The night conspires, oh what a sight!

The world may think it's all just fluff,
But who needs grace when you're this tough?
A misplaced charm upon a shoe,
Turns every glance to laughter's brew.

Dark corners hide the cheeky glee,
Where starlit pranks seem wild and free.
A snicker here, a jabber there,
As elegance thrums in midnight air.

So toast the oddities we seek,
As whispers weave a tale unique.
In murky depths, we find our spark,
With laughter dancing in the dark.

Reflections on Velvet

On velvet nights, the giggles slip,
With treasures shared from a daring trip.
A look around, a cheeky grin,
In shadows deep, let chaos win.

The elegance of clumsiness reigns,
As laughter breaks through all the chains.
A precious gem that dashed away,
Turns to fun in the light of play.

With every glance, a story brews,
The sparkles lead to silly views.
What's lost in dark becomes a jest,
That turns the night into a fest.

So gather round with joyful cheers,
And toast to mischief through the years.
For velvet nights don't last for long,
Let laughter guide us, bright and strong.

Nocturnal Opus

In moonlit realms of foolish pride,
The hidden sparkles seem to hide.
With every chuckle shared at night,
A symphony of joy takes flight.

A clattering sound, a shoe that slips,
A treasure floats beyond our grips.
The shadows clutch their giggling sake,
As laughter's tune begins to quake.

The dark reveals a winking jest,
Where elegance avoids the best.
A heist that turns to cheeks ablaze,
In playful tricks we find our ways.

So let the stars join in our song,
As we embrace what feels so wrong.
With every giggle, bravely sung,
In nocturnal dreams, we are so young!

Glistening Hues of the Abyss

In a bag of treasures, oh so bright,
A rogue raccoon danced with delight.
He tried on bracelets, rings with glee,
What a sight! What a spree!

Under the moon, he pranced around,
While lost in laughter, he fell to the ground.
His sparkly loot scattered everywhere,
Oh dear raccoon, pause for a prayer!

Each glimmering piece, a laugh in disguise,
As he winked at stars, with mischievous eyes.
In the shadows, they giggled and gleamed,
Life's a party, or so it seemed!

In the depths where the oddities play,
Even a thief can have a bright day.
With mirrors and jewels, he made his mark,
The hyena chuckled, "A true work of art!"

Shadows Cradling Sparkling Dreams

In the velvet night, a bubble of fun,
A parrot squawked, "I'm second to none!"
His beak adorned with gems of the night,
Who knew a bird could have such height?

He flew through the alley, with such flair,
Stealing the limelight and some silly air.
"Oh look at me!" he sang with a twist,
Who knew a pirate could dance like this?

Through darkened paths, he led a parade,
With shadows that twinkled, a glorious charade.
The creatures gathered, their hearts full of cheer,
With a blinged-out bird, full of good beer!

They danced on the rooftops, a marvelous sight,
Each glow and each giggle, pure delight.
When morning arrived, they scattered away,
Leaving sparkle behind—what a wild day!

Dusk's Hidden Opulence

As twilight fell, the silly mice crept,
In search of a treasure, the kind to be kept.
With tiny hats on their heads, each wore,
They swaggered right up to the glittering door.

Behind velvet curtains, they sought and they sought,
Till a goofy old shoe brought them luck—who'd have thought?
It shimmered like gold, a sight very rare,
"Let's fill it with cheese!" they shouted with flair!

A raccoon's lost stash brought laughter afloat,
With diamonds and trinkets in this worn-out coat.
The mice threw a ball, in shoes that danced light,
Underneath the moon, oh what a bright sight!

As dawn's first light peeked through the haze,
They left their marks with giggles and plays.
Each mouse in a shoe, proud and so spry,
Who knew living large could come from a pie?

Enigmas Wrapped in Silk

Amidst the shadows, a cat with finesse,
Wore pearls and ribbons, quite the mistress.
She strolled through the lane with her head held tall,
That regal feline—do we dare call?

The moonlight caressed her flowing coat,
While trinkets jingled around her throat.
"Catch me if you can!" purred she with a laugh,
As critters behind tried to find a path.

With a leap and a twirl, she danced through the park,
Leaving behind a giggling lark.
Her charisma was dazzling, oh what a show,
"A treasure to keep? Who knows where to go?"

Yet soon she grew tired of her glamorous game,
And dreamed of the comforts of a simple name.
Wrapped in the charm, she settled her head,
With silk and with dreams—what a world to be fed!

Nightfall's Enchantments

When twilight whispers and shadows sway,
The stars emerge in a playful ballet.
One sparkly gem lost under the bed,
Sparks laughter and dreams of adventures ahead.

A treasure once worn, now a mere jest,
In the fridge, it waits for an unlikely fest.
Glow of the moon makes it twinkle with glee,
Who knew the dark could be so carefree?

Old stories emerge as we giggle and peek,
At the mysteries hidden, shadows grow sleek.
With each little chuckle, a memory will rise,
The night's silly charm is a sweet surprise.

So dance in the twilight, let laughter take flight,
With trinkets of humor to make spirits bright.
In the glow of the dusk, let our joy take the helm,
In the magic of night, we craft our own realm.

Luminous Threads of Night

In the depth of the night, mischievous and spry,
A diamond's lost will make the whole room cry.
We search with a grin, through shadows we roam,
Finding tangled
threads of our laughter-filled home.

Glowing with secrets, the dark lends its flair,
As we trip on trinkets, tearing through air.
Oh! Just what a sight, a ring on the cat,
Adding to the drama, and how we all spat!

Through the whispers of night, the humor unfolds,
A sparkly adventure like nothing foretold.
In our patchwork of dreams, every giggle takes flight,
In luminous threads that weave through the night.

So gather the glow of mishaps and cheer,
With each little sparkle, there's nothing to fear.
As the night hugs the chaos, we'll dance in delight,
For we are the jesters, basking in twilight.

Treasures Across the Gloom

Amidst the shadows, treasures hide,
A glint of a charm that tickles with pride.
We stumble and fumble, big grins on our face,
In the gloom of the night, we find our place.

A bracelet once lost takes on a new lane,
On the dog, it jingles, a comical gain.
While searching for gems, silly antics ensue,
Our shadows are partners in the laughter we brew.

As the moon plays its tricks, our spirits feel light,
With every misstep, we conjure a flight.
The night's whimsical gift, a jest so divine,
Each sparkle reminds us that laughter will shine.

So here in the dark, we'll cherish the breeze,
With each hidden treasure that makes us feel pleased.
The gloom holds its secrets, and we'll giggle along,
Creating our ballad, our own midnight song.

Charmed in the Shadowlight

The dark holds the dreams of a whimsical night,
Where trinkets enchanted dance with delight.
An earring misplaced is a tale on its own,
In the charm of mishaps, our laughter is grown.

With sparkly glasses and hats tipped askew,
We wander the shadows and giggle anew.
The moon chuckles softly as we leap and we sway,
In the magic of mischief, we find our own way.

Lost baubles and sparks, what a colorful spree,
Like chameleons playing through shadows we see.
With every odd twist, our joy takes a cue,
For the enchantment of night is in all that we do.

So play through the twilight, in jovial flight,
With treasures of laughter to share through the night.
In the glow of our chaos, we're charmingly bright,
As we twirl in the shadows, our spirits take flight.

Enigmatic Radiance

In shadows cast, a glimmer shines,
A spark of joy in tangled lines.
I lost my bling in a game of dice,
Now every laugh feels like a slice.

A trinket lost, but jokes are free,
I wore my humor like a spree.
With every stumble, I find my way,
Laughter's the prize at the end of the day.

A mystery wrapped in giggles bright,
Fumbling around in the soft moonlight.
A search for treasure, yet what's the cost?
Those fancy things may not be lost.

So here's the truth, much to my surprise,
The real jewels are found in laughter's rise.
With every blooper, a story unfolds,
A dazzling veiled wealth that never grows old.

Threads of Enchantment

Tangled tales of hidden gems,
A stash of secrets, and whimsical trends.
With every thread, a giggle weaves,
A tapestry of laughter that never leaves.

Once misplaced, my sparkle blazed,
Through midnight quests, I felt quite fazed.
Yet every oops and every spill,
Turns into humor, a delightful thrill.

Lost and found, that's how it goes,
In darkened corners, my humor glows.
A dance of shadows, a funny spree,
Chasing lost charms just to feel free.

So raise a glass to all that's bright,
In the chase of fun, we find our light.
With every twist and every twist,
The magic lies in the laughter missed.

Luster Lost and Found

A glint once gleamed on the floor,
It's now a memory, who keeps score?
In shoes too tight, I trip and roll,
Yet laughter echoes, filling the hole.

Chasing shadows, I stumble wide,
A treasure hunt with no great pride.
But every slip becomes a joke,
As friends and I in giggles choke.

Luster lost, oh what a shame,
Yet I laugh hard at my own little game.
In the dark, we twirl and dance,
Finding joy in each mischance.

So here's to laughter, bright and bold,
With every chuckle, my heart turns gold.
No gem can match the fun we find,
In memories shared and tales entwined.

Midnight's Hidden Wealth

In midnight's realm, where secrets lurk,
I fumble and bumble like a silly jerk.
Searching for treasures, but find only glee,
A fortune of laughter awaits, you see.

Lost a bauble in a late-night chat,
But who needs diamonds when you're this fat?
With every story we spin and tell,
Our joy rings louder than any church bell.

In shadows deep, the fun comes alive,
A treasure chest where our giggles thrive.
So while I quest for that shiny bit,
I may just stick with this joke, it's a hit!

With every hiccup, a laugh we unearth,
In midnight's dance, we celebrate worth.
So come join the fun, let your heart swell,
In this playful dig, we all do well.

Radiant Mysteries Encased in Night

In shadows deep, a glimmer glows,
A playful spark, where nobody knows.
Twirls and giggles, the moonlight beams,
Who needs a crown? We've got wild dreams.

A wink of silver, a dash of flair,
Stolen moments, without a care.
Riddles hide in laughter's chase,
With every turn, a silly face.

A treasure found in the darkest guise,
Hiding mischief behind tired eyes.
Let's dance with glee and steal the night,
Wrapped in fun, it feels so right.

So join the whimsy, take a chance,
In perfect chaos, we shall dance.
For laughter's shine will guide the way,
In this funny world, we'll laugh and play.

A Hidden Brilliance

In the attic's gloom, a sparkle winks,
It's not a ghost, just a spark that thinks.
It hums and jiggles as we all stare,
Elusive charm wrapped up in flair.

The evening hums with playful cheer,
A hidden jewel brings us near.
Under the bed, it starts to play,
Chasing shadows, brightening the gray.

Whispers of laughter fill the air,
What's that shine? A strange affair!
Giggling secrets in every nook,
A silly game in this shadowed book.

In laughter's arms, the night unfolds,
A jester's heart in whispers bold.
For in the dark, we're truly bright,
With dreams aglow, we own the night.

Locket of the Night's Heart

Beneath the stars, a spark so sly,
Winks at the moon as we pass by.
With each heartbeat, it tells a tale,
Of mystery wrapped in laughter's veil.

A playful jest and flicker of light,
Hiding treasures in the night.
What's that twinkling? A cheeky tease,
Laughter escaping on the cool breeze.

Shadows dance to a silly tune,
The world's a stage under the moon.
With every giggle, the ribbons twine,
In this locket, a spark divine.

Embrace this jest; hold on tight,
For joy is found in the softest light.
In hidden corners, the fun starts to part,
As we unlock the night's bright heart.

Secrets Wrapped in Silk

In layers of silk, secrets do play,
Tumbling forth in a cheeky way.
With every twist, a giggle ignites,
As shadows spin under soft moonlight.

A playful riddle dressed in dreams,
We chase the laughter, hear the screams.
What's that shimmer? A whispering clue,
Unfolding wonders both old and new.

Tangled up in this web so fine,
We share smiles over sweetened wine.
For in the dark, we find such mirth,
Each secret brings us closer to Earth.

So let's unwrap this joyful pack,
With laughter's gift we'll never lack.
In silk's embrace, we're wrapped in glee,
Creating a world where we're truly free.

Silhouettes of Forgotten Luxury

In shadows where treasures once gleamed bright,
A dog poses grand in the pale moonlight.
With a collar of dreams, or so he believes,
He struts through the park, causing a few reprieves.

A lady in pearls, her eyes all aglow,
Trips on her heels, puts on quite the show.
"Alas!" she declares, "This fashion is cruel!"
While dogs chase the squirrels, she feels like a fool.

The remnants of parties, where laughter reigns true,
Are now just a memory, of chaos askew.
She fumbles her jewels, they scatter around,
"Look at this mess! It's a crown I have found!"

Yet in the moon's gaze, the farcical dance,
Of a lady and pup, ignites a strange chance.
With every odd twirl, a chuckle erupts,
For who needs the wealth, when joy interrupts?

The Allure of Hidden Lights

Glittering stars sigh, with secrets so bold,
They whisper of paths paved with riches untold.
A raccoon in shades, with a thief's sharp finesse,
Scours through the trash, claiming glamour, no less.

Old shoes strung with sequins, above in a tree,
Tangled in laughter, just waiting for glee.
A squirrel dons pearls, with a flick of its tail,
As it fashions a crown, and begins to regale.

The glow of a lantern, a candle misplaced,
Reveals sparkling truths, in the dark, interlaced.
With giggles and gasps, the moon winks with pride,
In the night's silly game, there's nowhere to hide.

When jewels of the past become tales of delight,
The bittersweet charm turns the shadows to light.
We dance in our banter, we wear our mistakes,
In the treasure of laughter, a legacy wakes.

Soliloquies of Night's Adornments

A cat in a collar, glittering and grand,
Struts through the dusk like the queen of the land.
With mischief in mind and a tip of her paw,
She enchants neighborhood mice, making them thaw.

There's a hat from last spring, on the fence it now hangs,
With ribbons and fluff, it's lost all its clangs.
But in midnight's embrace, it dances in glee,
Flaunting its moments, so proud to be free.

The whispers of fashion, in jest, draw us near,
As a couple of dogs don wigs, shedding fear.
With every soft howl, the moon rolls its eyes,
"Where's my red carpet, for these wild, funny flies?"

So let's toast to the night, where silliness blooms,
Where fashion lies scattered, in laughter-filled rooms.
For in this grand chaos, we find something bright,
In the soliloquies spun by the essence of night.

The Allure of Concealed Splendor

In the attic she stumbles, through dust and regret,
Finds a box full of treasures, no need to fret.
Old hats and a brooch, all coated with clay,
She tries on the sparkle, and twirls in her sway.

A mirror reflects all the giggles at night,
As she dons every piece, feeling whimsical light.
"Oh look at me!" she exclaims with delight,
"I'm a star of the show, so dazzling and bright!"

A gust of the wind blows her plans to dismay,
As her jewels take flight, like they're wanting to play.
They roll down the sidewalk, like rhymes running loose,
Each twinkling laughter, a fun little truce.

Yet there in the moonlight, as chaos unfolds,
She learns hidden splendor is more than just gold.
With each laugh and blunder, she finds her own charm,
In the allure of the night, she discovers her warm.

Moonlit Treasure

In shadows cast by silver beams,
A trinket sparkles, or so it seems.
The cat thinks it's a diamond bright,
But it's just a button found last night.

The owls hoot with an air of glee,
As mice dance, curiously carefree.
A blingy bauble, lost and tossed,
Who needs riches? Oh, what a cost!

With every step, owls throw a cheer,
While I trip over—my balance severe.
In this chaos, I laugh till I ache,
For the fun of the hunt, I won't forsake.

So here's to treasures not worth a dime,
That bring us laughter time after time.
In moonlit nights, we search with delight,
For quirky wonders hidden from sight.

Veiled Splendor

A shimmery sight beneath the fluff,
I swear it's gold, but it's just a cuff.
Wrapped in mystery, or is it fate?
A tale of bling that's second-rate.

The dog thinks it's a ball of fate,
Chasing dreams that glitter too late.
I make my stand, proud and so bold,
In the realm of shiny, just pure gold!

Yet, in the hunt, hilarity flows,
For no one knows where this treasure goes.
A rogue raccoon with a style so grand,
Steals my sparkle, plays the band!

So let the night hold glittered jest,
In the world of whimsy, I've found the best.
With laughter echoing, our hearts so light,
We cherish the dark, all cheerful and bright.

Echoing Gemstones

In a box of odds, a mystery shines,
A clattering treasure, with no clear signs.
The socks claim jewels in a hidden lair,
While I trip over slippers, unaware!

A clink of laughter with each misplaced prize,
The mirror reflects my wide-open eyes.
What's that sparkle? Perhaps a lost ring,
Nope! Just a cap, but oh, what a thing!

The shadows whisper tales of the night,
As I dance solo, giving a fright.
With glimmers of hope in a headstand I make,
This treasure hunt's a whimsical quake!

So here's to the gems that never truly are,
In a whimsical world, they shine like a star.
Each echoing laugh gets brighter in tune,
As the treasures of darkness bloom under the moon.

Dazzling Desires in Dim Light

In dim light, a sparkle, what do I see?
A craving for treasure, just wild, just free.
A carnival ride, full of flair,
Or maybe it's just the dog's shiny hair!

Whispers of fortune dance in the air,
What's next, a disco? A treasure to share?
With dreams of diamonds and silly delight,
I stumble away, giggling into the night.

Each twinkling thought is a wish that we chase,
In the shadows, we find our own funny place.
It's not always gold that will catch our eye,
But memories spun in a giggly sigh.

So let shiny dreams guide our playful plight,
With laughter ignited in soft dim light.
In search of more than a glimmering prize,
We find the true treasure is laughter that flies.

The Allure Beneath Stars

In shadows where the whispers play,
A hidden treasure leads astray,
With laughter in the midnight dawn,
And every wish she boldly fawn.

A dazzling twinkle, oh so bright,
Makes every clumsy move feel right,
She stumbles, fumbles with a grin,
The mirthful dance about to begin.

A cardboard box, her secret prize,
She swaggers 'neath the velvet skies,
And every star, a knowing wink,
While others wonder what to think.

But in the morning's harshest light,
The glimmer fades from sheer delight,
Yet in her heart, a spark remains,
Of silly antics, joy, and gains.

Gleam of the Unseen

A glint of gold in streetlight's glow,
Her antics start a lively show,
In absent dreams of riches bold,
A tale of laughter to be told.

The mirror laughs back with a grin,
Each facet buzzing with a spin,
"Just one more cocktail, let's pretend!"
As heads keep nodding, none descend.

Around her neck, a twist of fate,
A playful charm that's sure to date,
While friends all murmur and they tease,
"Is this the charm that brings us trees?"

She dances under twinkling moons,
Ignoring all the absent tunes,
For every silly thing she wears,
Becomes a treasure of her cares.

Faded Glories

In dusty boxes lies her flair,
With vintage style beyond compare,
The laughter echoes, memories bloom,
A glitter's shine amid the gloom.

Once lustrous gems, now tales from youth,
She tells each one, naive, uncouth,
Her friends all giggle, roll their eyes,
As tales evolve into wild lies.

In every party, bold and grand,
She juggles truths with steady hand,
"Remember that? Oh what a night!"
As friends all nod, with face alight.

Yet time moves on, and so must she,
Each faded glory, a mystery,
The laughter stays as sparkle fades,
In heart and mind, the music spades.

Gems of Forgotten Memory

Beneath the pile of old attire,
She finds a glimmer to inspire,
For every piece, a crafted tale,
Of silly mischief, laughter's trail.

The jeweled pin with chipped enamel,
Encapsulates a wild camel,
Or better yet—a frisky dance,
With buddy, and her sparkly chance.

Yet all the stories twisted tight,
She wears her past with sheer delight,
As if to say, "Each gem's the key,
To joy and adult history."

And when the sun begins to set,
She stands adorned with no regret,
For every laugh, a timeless gem,
That sparkles bright, her diadem.

The Lurking Glamour

In shadows where the sparkles play,
A treasure hides in bright array.
Yet glamour's grin is just a tease,
It plays at splendor, if you please.

A glint of gold in dim-lit rooms,
With laughter loud, it seeks its dooms.
A flash of jewels, they make us sigh,
But in a blink, they're just a lie.

With every twinkle, folly reigns,
It dances lightly, skips the chains.
In corners dark, chortles abound,
Oh, playful glimmers, never found!

So hold your breath and laugh away,
For tricks of light can lead astray.
When charm is just a rogue masquerade,
The lurking, laughing, fun parade!

Shimmering in the Abyss

In depths unseen, a shine resides,
With winks and giggles, joy abides.
A splash of flair, a wink of fate,
The shimmer's here; don't hesitate!

A dance of sparkles, oh so bright,
In eerie places, pure delight.
They tease the heart, a little fun,
As shadows waltz, they've truly won.

The glow might fade, or so they say,
Yet still we laugh and hope they stay.
An echo echoes, "What's the catch?"
But foolish hearts just love to match!

So play along in this dark game,
For what's the joy if it's not lame?
We twirl and spin, just take a chance,
In shimmering light, we find our dance!

Whispers of Hidden Luxury

In hushed tones, the jewels conspire,
With rhymes and giggles, never tire.
They whisper secrets, sly and sweet,
Pretending that they're quite a treat.

A glimmer here, a chuckle there,
In corners where the folks don't care.
With humor wrapped in velvet lies,
They twinkle brightly, craft disguise.

Each sparkle hides a jest or two,
With every glance, a silly view.
As laughter dances with the light,
We jest with pearls, all in goodnight.

So listen well, for jokes abound,
In luxury where laughs are found.
With whispers low and spirits high,
We find our joy beneath the sky!

Radiance Wrapped in Mystique

A dazzle's tale in night's embrace,
Where every shine finds silly space.
Wrapped in charm, oh what a sight,
    Dancing bold in velvet night.

The mystery twirls, a playful tease,
With chuckles soft as evening breeze.
Hidden gems with winks so bright,
    Wrap us tight in pure delight.

Luminous whispers weave and spin,
    An echo of the fun within.
Something sparkling meets the eye,
    A laugh, a hint—oh me, oh my!

So let's embrace this gleeful show,
With shining truths we rarely know.
In radiance wrapped, let's all unite,
In mystique's grip, we feel just right!

Gemstones of Forgotten Tales

In a box all dusty and worn,
Lies a treasure, slightly forlorn.
Once a prize, now a joke,
A story of old, with no smoke.

It sparkled bright at a fancy ball,
Now it's just an overly bold brawl.
Rattling around, with a life of its own,
Who knew such weight could make one moan?

Its shimmer caught a cat's sly eye,
He pounced and slipped—oh my, oh my!
Chasing shadows, he bumped the light,
A clattering dance, what a silly sight!

So here's to treasures, lost in a heap,
They may look fancy, but make us weep.
In laughter and chaos, a gem may shine,
For beauty often dwells where the whimsies intertwine.

Glimmering Secrets in Twilight

A bauble gleamed beneath the bed,
Caught a ghost with a glimmering head.
It whispered tales of long-lost rain,
And made us giggle, forgetting the pain.

With twinkling eyes and a sly little grin,
It told us of parties where no one could win.
Dancing and prancing in shadows so deep,
All while we laughed until we fell asleep.

A trinket of humor, brushed off the dust,
'Oh look!' it said, 'in me, you can trust!'
But wearing it out brought such a fuss,
Wherever I went, mischief must discuss.

So let us cherish the secrets they weave,
In peculiar moments, what to believe?
With laughter and joy, we dive in the night,
Finding glimmering secrets that make our hearts light.

The Soft Glow of Hidden Treasures

In a drawer full of odds and ends,
Lay a glow that broke all trends.
A pendant, once cherished, turned absurd,
Worn by the snoozing, midnight bird.

Its shine caressed our laughter so bright,
The cat mistook it for a ball in flight.
With a swat and a scratch, it danced in the dark,
Creating a ruckus with every little spark.

"Oh, don't mind me," it chuckled with glee,
"I'm just here for the fun and the party, you see!"
With each little twink, all bravely began,
To spin through the night like some whimsical fan.

So let us rejoice in the glow of the night,
Hidden treasures can bring pure delight.
In garish absurdity, laughter will flow,
As we prance with the glow, loving the show.

Silhouettes of Elegance

In the dark, there danced a shape,
Wearing gems that looked like cake.
With a flick and a twist, it beckoned us near,
A clumsy ballet that sparked our cheer.

The classy silhouette wobbled with grace,
Each step a giggle, a grin on its face.
Chasing a glow that seemed all but fake,
Hoping to catch the light before a break.

Rushed to the gala, it tripped on a shoe,
Found itself stuck, oh what to do?
With a laugh, it bowed, made the crowd reel,
What a funny charm, making it all surreal.

So here's to the elegance we find in the night,
Where shadows play, and laughter ignites.
In silhouettes weird, let our spirits embark,
For in every jest, lives an eternal spark.

www.ingramcontent.com/pod-product-compliance
Lightning Source LLC
Chambersburg PA
CBHW060115230426
43661CB00003B/194